TABLE OF CONTENTS

T0058561

READY TO BLOW!

Earthquakes shake the ground. The air smells like rotten eggs. Steam pours from the top of a nearby mountain. This isn't just any mountain. It's a volcano ready to **erupt**!

WORLD'S WORST NATURAL DISASTERS

THE WORLD'S WORST
VOLCANIC
ERUPTIONS

by Tracy Nelson Maurer

CAPSTONE PRESS
a capstone imprint

Blazers Books are published by Capstone Press,
1710 Roe Crest Drive, North Mankato, Minnesota 56003
www.mycapstone.com

Library of Congress Cataloging-in-Publication Data is available on the
Library of Congress website.
ISBN: 978-1-5435-5480-9 (library hardcover) — 978-1-5435-5904-0
(paperback) — 978-1-5435-5484-7 (eBook PDF)

Summary: Provides information on the most devastating volcanic
eruptions in history.

Editorial Credits
Gena Chester, editor; Juliette Peters, designer; Jo Miller,
media researcher; Tori Abraham, production specialist

Photo Credits
Alamy: FAY 2018, 18–19; AP Images: Pat Roque, 12–13; Bridgeman
Images: Private Collection/Look and Learn, 26–27; Dreamstime:
George Burba, Cover; Getty Images: Apic/RETIRED/Contributor,
8–9, Langevin Jacques/Contributor, 16–17; Mary Evans Picture
Library: Sueddeutsche Zeitung Photo, 10–11; Newscom: VWPics/
Francois Gohler, 14–15, ZUMA Press/C. Dan Miller, 20–21; Science
Source: Prof. Stewart Lowther, 6–7; Shutterstock: balounm, 24–25,
fboudrias, 4–5, leonello calvetti, Cover, 3, 31, peresanz, 22–23,
Pete Niesen, 28–29

Design Elements
Shutterstock: fboudrias, Ivana Milic, xpixel

VEI SCALE

Scientists use the Volcanic Explosivity Index (VEI) to measure an eruption. Each eruption rates a number from 0 (small) to 8 (huge).

VEI:

0

1

2

3

4

5

6

7

8

FACT Earth's last VEI 8 happened about 27,000 years ago in New Zealand.

erupt—to burst out suddenly with great force

HOW VOLCANOES ERUPT

Some volcanoes erupt slowly. **Magma** oozes out and gives people time to escape. Other volcanoes have explosive eruptions. Magma rumbles deep beneath the earth. Then earthquakes shake the magma, like soda in a bottle. The pressure sends **lava**, **toxic** gas, and ash out of the volcano.

magma—melted rock found beneath the earth's surface
lava—the hot, liquid rock that pours out of a volcano when it erupts
toxic—poisonous

DEADLIEST 20TH-CENTURY ERUPTION

Location:
Mount Pelée,
Martinique

Date:
May 8, 1902

VEI: 4

0
1
2
3
4 ◄
5
6
7
8

Mount Pelée's eruption in 1902 destroyed the town of St. Pierre, Martinique. Deadly gas and ash rushed down the volcano's peak at about 100 miles (161 kilometers) per hour. Almost 30,000 people died.

FACT

On May 7th, a volcano on an island near Mount Pelée also erupted. It killed 1,500 people.

RECORD BREAKER

Location:
Mount Tambora,
Indonesia

Date:
April 5–10, 1815

VEI: 7

0
1
2
3
4
5
6
7 ◄
8

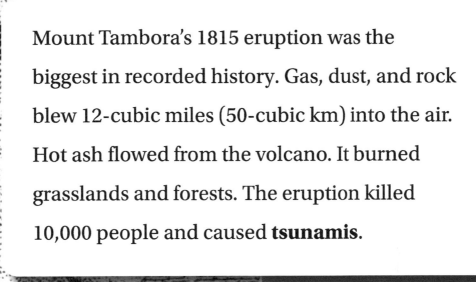

Mount Tambora's 1815 eruption was the biggest in recorded history. Gas, dust, and rock blew 12-cubic miles (50-cubic km) into the air. Hot ash flowed from the volcano. It burned grasslands and forests. The eruption killed 10,000 people and caused **tsunamis**.

FACT

Together, the tsunami and the eruption killed about 38,000 people.

tsunami—a large, destructive wave caused by an underwater earthquake or volcano

AMAZING EVACUATIONS

Location:
Mount Pinatubo,
Philippines

Date:
June 15, 1991

VEI: 6

0
1
2
3
4
5
6 ◀
7
8

FACT

Mount Pinatubo spread ash 22 miles (35 km). It reached neighboring villages and U.S. Clark Air Base.

Modern science saved lives when Mount Pinatubo erupted in 1991. Scientists saw the warning signs that the volcano was about to blow. They told people to **evacuate**. As many as 20,000 people listened. Still, about 300 people lost their lives.

evacuate—to leave an area during a time of danger

HOT HAWAIIAN TOPIC

Location:
Kilauea Volcano,
the Big Island of
Hawaii, USA

Date:
May 3, 2018

VEI: 1

0
1 ◄
2
3
4
5
6
7
8

The world's most active volcano is Kilauea. Hot lava has oozed from it since 1983. On May 3, 2018, new openings in the ground created fresh paths for lava flow. No one knows when the eruption will end.

Volcanoes made each of the Hawaiian Islands. Only the volcanoes Kilauea and Mauna Loa are still active.

KILLER RIVER

Location:
Nevado del Ruiz
Volcano, Colombia

Date:
November 13, 1985

VEI: 3

0
1
2
3 ◄
4
5
6
7
8

The Nevado del Ruiz Volcano erupted in 1985. Heat from the eruption melted mountain snow and ice. The water mixed with volcanic ash and mud. It flooded the town of Armero. About 25,000 people died.

FACT

Most of the world's volcanoes border the Pacific Ocean. This area of volcanoes and earthquake activity is called "The Ring of Fire."

SOUTH AMERICA'S WORST VOLCANO

Location:
Huaynaputina
Volcano, Peru

Date:
February 19, 1600

VEI: 6

0
1
2
3
4
5
6 ◄
7
8

Huaynaputina surprised everyone when the powerful volcano erupted in 1600. Hot mudflows reached the Pacific Ocean, 75 miles (120 km) away. It is the largest known eruption in South America.

DEADLY ERUPTION IN THE USA

Location:
Mount St. Helens,
Washington, USA

Date:
May 18, 1980

VEI: 5

0
1
2
3
4
5
6
7 ◄
8

Mount St. Helens erupted in a big way in 1980. The north side of the mountain blew off! It caused a massive **landslide**. The eruption killed 57 people.

The air blast from Mount St. Helens' eruption tore down trees within 200 square miles (518 square km).

landslide—a large mass of earth and rocks that suddenly slides down a mountain or hill

SUPERVOLCANO COUNTDOWN

Location:
Yellowstone National Park, Wyoming, USA

Date:
640,000 years ago

VEI: 8

0
1
2
3
4
5
6
7
8 ◄

Yellowstone has had three VEI 8 eruptions. The last one was 640,000 years ago. If the supervolcano were to erupt again, ash could reach as far as the Atlantic Ocean. Scientists watch for signs of another big eruption to help warn people in time.

FACT

The magma underneath Yellowstone could fill the Grand Canyon 11 times.

BURIED FOR CENTURIES

Location:
Mount Vesuvius,
Italy

Date:
August 24, 79 CE

VEI: 5

0
1
2
3
4
5 ◄
6
7
8

Almost 2,000 years ago, Mount Vesuvius gushed hot ash, rock, and toxic gas. The hot volcanic flow killed people instantly in the cities of Pompeii and Herculaneum. Their bodies were **preserved** in volcanic ash until they were discovered about 1,700 years later.

FACT

A man named Pliny the Younger saw Vesuvius erupt. He later wrote down what he saw. Today the biggest and most powerful type of eruption, plinian, is named after him.

preserved—something that has stayed in its original condition

plinian—a large volcanic eruption in which gas, ash, and volcanic rock is sent high into the air

WHAT'S THAT SOUND?

Location:
Krakatoa,
Indonesia

Date:
August 26, 1883

VEI: 6

0
1
2
3
4
5
6 ◄
7
8

Multiple explosions rocked the island of Krakatoa in 1883. They were heard up to 2,200 miles (3,500 km) away. Only a few people died from the eruption. But the blasts also set off tsunamis, which hit many nearby islands. Around 36,000 people drowned.

FACT

The ash from the eruption completely covered Krakatoa. It took five years for plant and animal life to fully return to the island.

STAY AWAY

DANGER

DO NOT ENTER
_____

AREA
CLOSED

**Land Beyond This Point
Is Closed To Public Use
Due To Volcanic Hazards
Authorized Persons Only**

VIOLATORS SUBJECT TO FINE: 36 CFR 1.5 (A)(1)

UNITED STATES DEPARTMENT OF THE INTERIOR   NATIONAL PARK SERVICE

Scientists cannot say exactly when a volcano will erupt. They cannot **prevent** eruptions. Stay away from active volcanoes to stay safe. If you live near an active volcano, these are some tips to keep in mind:

1. Have an emergency plan in case of an eruption.
2. Make a safety kit. Include a flashlight, battery-operated radio, goggles, and masks to protect your lungs from ash.
3. Keep windows and doors closed to stop ash from getting inside.

prevent—to keep from happening

GLOSSARY

erupt (i-RUHPT)—to burst out suddenly with great force

evacuate (i-VA-kyuh-wayt)—to leave an area during a time of danger

landslide (LAND-slyde)—a large mass of earth and rocks that suddenly slides down a mountain or hill

lava (LAH-vuh)—the hot, liquid rock that pours out of a volcano when it erupts

magma (MAG-muh)—melted rock found beneath the earth's surface

plinian (plihn-NEE-ihn)—a large volcanic eruption in which gas, ash, and volcanic rock is sent high into the air

preserved (pru-SERVD)—something that has stayed in its original condition

prevent (pri-VENT)—to keep from happening

toxic (TOK-sik)—poisonous

tsunami (tsoo-NAH-mee)—a large, destructive wave caused by an underwater earthquake or volcano

READ MORE

Ganeri, Anita. *Eruption!: The Story of Volcanoes.* New York: DK Publishing, 2015.

Meister, Cari. *Volcanoes.* Minneapolis: Jump!, Inc., 2016.

Squire, Ann. *Volcanic Eruptions.* New York: Scholastic, 2016.

INTERNET SITES

Use Facthound to find Internet sites related to this book.

Visit www.facthound.com.

Just type in 9781543554809 and go!

Check out projects, games and lots more at
www.capstonekids.com

CRITICAL THINKING QUESTIONS

1. How do volcanoes erupt?

2. When volcanic ash in the air blocks the sun for weeks, what might happen to the temperature? What might happen to plant life?

3. What is an eruption called when ash, gas, and volcanic rock are sent high into the air?

INDEX